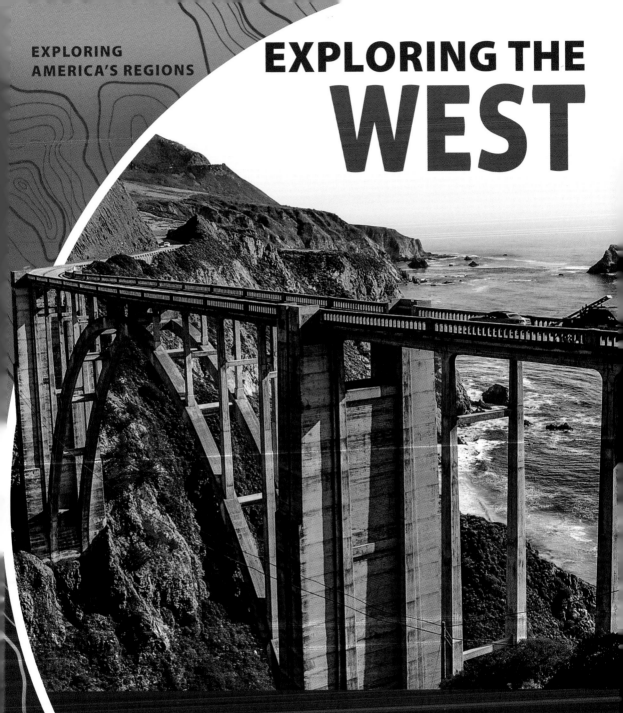

EXPLORING
AMERICA'S REGIONS

EXPLORING THE
WEST

BY ANITA YASUDA

CONTENT CONSULTANT
Jason LaBau, PhD
History Teacher
The Waterford School

Core Library

An Imprint of Abdo Publishing
abdopublishing.com

Cover image: The Big Sur region along California's
coast is rugged and mountainous.

abdopublishing.com

Published by Abdo Publishing, a division of ABDO, PO Box 398166, Minneapolis, Minnesota 55439. Copyright © 2018 by Abdo Consulting Group, Inc. International copyrights reserved in all countries. No part of this book may be reproduced in any form without written permission from the publisher. Core Library™ is a trademark and logo of Abdo Publishing.

Printed in the United States of America, North Mankato, Minnesota
092017
012018

Cover Photo: Shutterstock Images
Interior Photos: Shutterstock Images, 1, 7, 20, 45; Randal Sedler/Shutterstock Images, 4–5, 43; Red Line Editorial, 8, 31; Yaacov Dagan/Alamy, 10–11; North Wind Picture Archives, 13; Christopher Boswell/Shutterstock Images, 16–17; Julie Vader/Shutterstock Images, 22–23; Matthew Harrington/Shutterstock Images, 25; Rich Reid/National Geographic/Getty Images, 28–29; Andy Cross/Denver Post/Getty Images, 33; Benny Marty/Shutterstock Images, 34; Angel Wynn/ Danita Delimont/Alamy, 36–37

Editor: Maddie Spalding
Imprint Designer: Maggie Villaume
Series Design Direction: Ryan Gale

Publisher's Cataloging-in-Publication Data

Names: Yasuda, Anita, author.
Title: Exploring the West / by Anita Yasuda.
Description: Minneapolis, Minnesota : Abdo Publishing, 2018. | Series: Exploring America's regions | Includes online resources and index.
Identifiers: LCCN 2017946944 | ISBN 9781532113857 (lib.bdg.) | ISBN 9781532152733 (ebook)
Subjects: LCSH: West (U.S.)--Juvenile literature. | Discovery and exploration--Juvenile literature. | Travel--Juvenile literature. | United States--Historical geography--Juvenile literature.
Classification: DDC 917.8--dc23
LC record available at https://lccn.loc.gov/2017946944

CONTENTS

CHAPTER
ONE

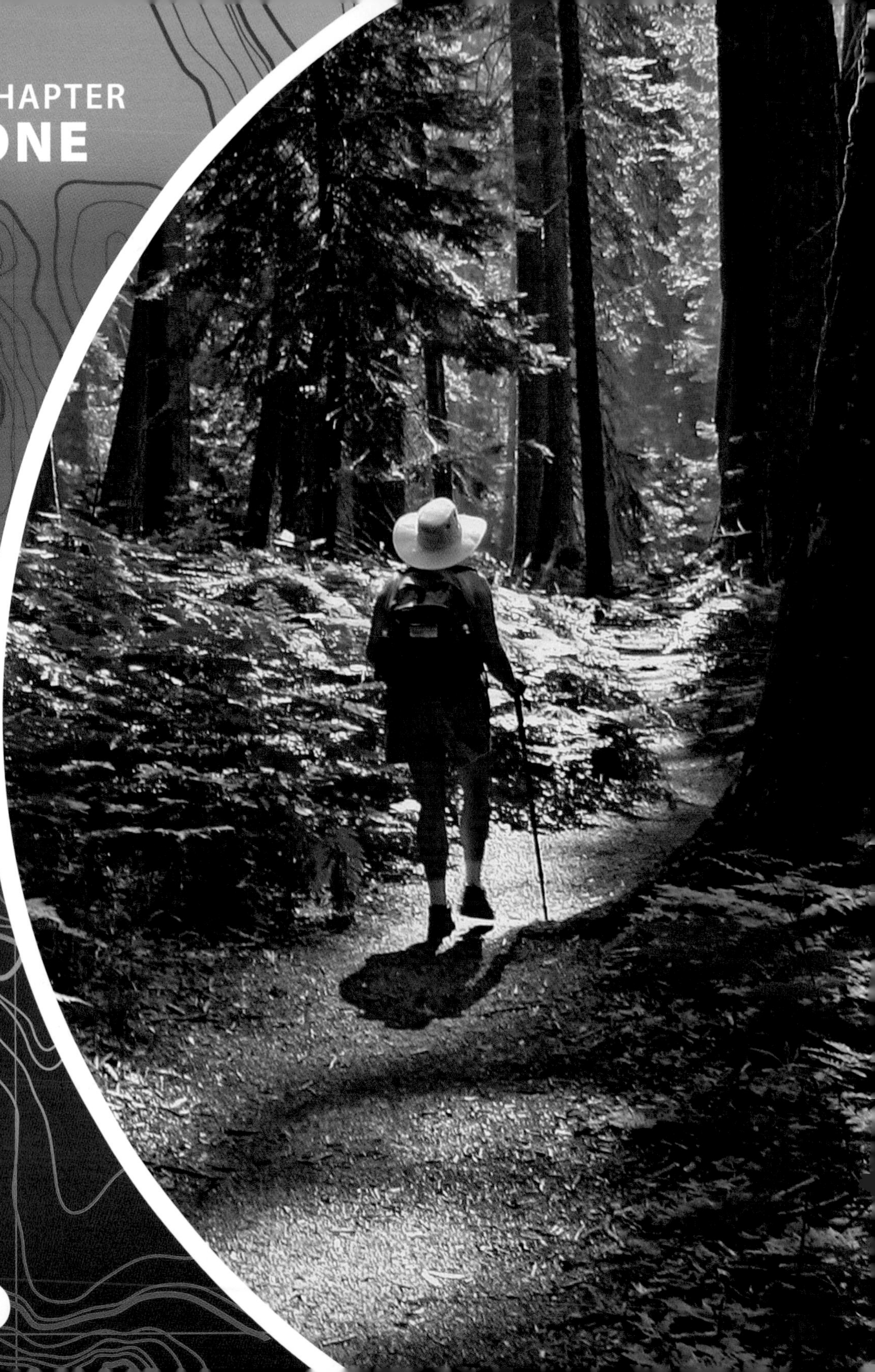

ACROSS THE GREAT WEST

The West has lots of wide, open spaces and incredible beauty. Along the jagged Pacific Coast, people may swim or leap through the surf. Further inland, visitors can climb some of the highest peaks in the United States. They can hike in vast deserts. There are hidden waterfalls in canyons to find. There are even areas with volcanoes to see.

ALL ABOUT SIZE

The West is the largest region in the United States. There are 11 states in this region. On the Pacific side are Washington, Oregon, and California. To the north, separated from

A hiker explores Sequoia National Park in California.

THE TROPICAL STATE

Hawaii is warm all year long. The ocean keeps the climate at a steady temperature. From May to October, temperatures average approximately 85 degrees Fahrenheit (29°C). From November to April, the weather is cooler, with temperatures around 78 degrees Fahrenheit (26°C). A lot of rain falls in the mountains. Mount Waialeale is one of the wettest places in the world. It is on the island of Kauai. It receives 450 inches (1,143 cm) of rain each year.

the other states by Canada, is Alaska. On the east side are Nevada, Idaho, Montana, Utah, Wyoming, and Colorado. The islands of Hawaii lie thousands of miles off the coast in the Pacific Ocean.

Seven of the top ten biggest US states are in the West. Alaska is the largest. But it has the third-smallest population of any state. Approximately 740,000 people live in Alaska. California has the largest population. More than 39 million people live there. The state is home to the second-largest city in the country, Los Angeles. It has nearly 4 million people.

Nevada has a dry desert climate.

THE CLIMATE OF THE WEST

The West has various climate zones. Winters along the Pacific Coast are usually cool and foggy. Some areas are very wet. Seattle, Washington, is one of the wettest cities in the United States. The climates of California, Nevada, and Montana are much hotter and drier. Las Vegas, Nevada, is one of the driest cities in the country. Only approximately 4 inches (10 cm) of rain fall there each year.

Alaska has long winter days. The town of Barrow, Alaska, is above the Arctic Circle. It does not see the sun all winter long. This is because Earth's axis is tilted.

THE WESTERN
REGION

This map highlights the western United States. After reading about the western region, what did you think it would look like? How does seeing the map help you better understand the size of this region?

During the winter, part of Earth tilts away from the sun. Some parts of Alaska are so cold that the ground remains frozen throughout much of the year.

The West's varied climates and landscapes draw thousands of people to the region each year. With so much to do and see, it is no wonder that the West is one of the most popular regions of the United States.

PERSPECTIVES
THE MODOC

The Modoc are a Native American tribe. They once lived along the border of California and Oregon. In the winter, groups of Modoc people lived near lakes. They hunted water birds such as ducks. Each spring, they moved near rivers to fish for salmon. They also gathered roots, berries, and fruits. Modoc author Cheewa James writes: "Modocs . . . did not see the land as something to be owned, any more than they saw owning the clouds."

In the 1800s, European settlers forced the Modoc from their lands. Today, the Modoc live on reservations in Oregon and Oklahoma.

CHAPTER
TWO

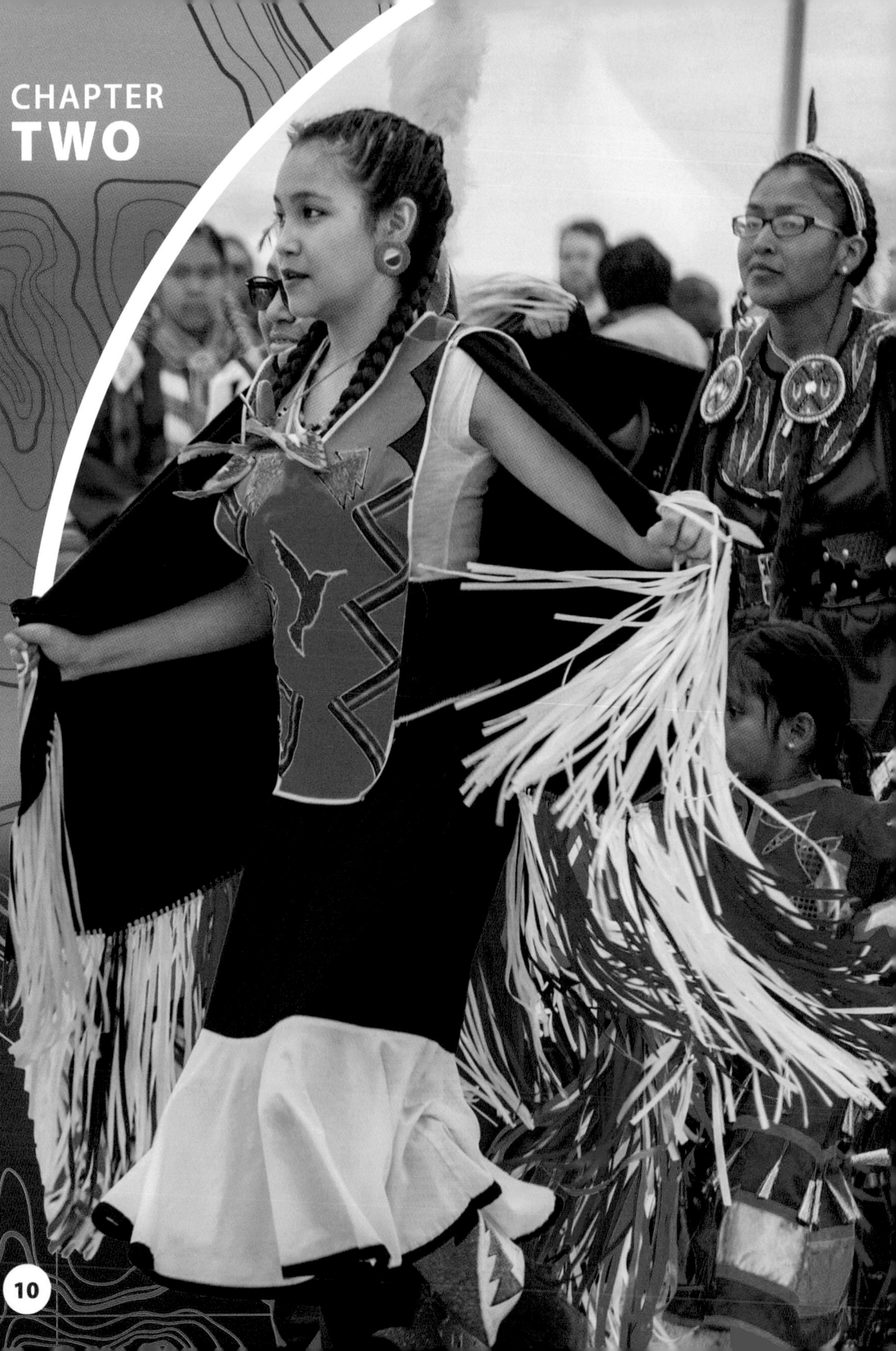

HISTORY AND SETTLEMENT

The West has a rich and complex history. Native Americans were the land's first occupants. The Unangan homelands are in present-day Alaska. There are approximately 2,000 Unangan people living in Alaska today.

Native American groups such as the Northern and Southern Paiute live farther south. Their lands once stretched from Oregon to Utah before European settlers came and drove them out. Today, some Paiute live on small reservations in Nevada and Utah.

Women perform a traditional dance at the annual Paiute Tribe Pow Wow in Las Vegas.

EXPANSION

In 1867, the United States purchased Alaska from Russia. Many Americans did not see why this region was important. But in World War II (1939–1945), this view changed. The US Army and Navy had bases here. Hawaii was also important during World War II. Hawaii had become a US territory in 1898. The United States used Pearl Harbor on the island of Oahu as a naval base. The bombing of Pearl Harbor in 1941 drew the United States into the war. On January 3, 1959, Alaska became the forty-ninth US state. Hawaii later became the fiftieth state on August 21, 1959.

THE GOLD RUSH

Gold was found in California in 1848. Settlers began to cross the country in large numbers. Native Americans had been living in the West for thousands of years. But these European settlers wanted to claim the lands as their own. They killed many Native Americans or forced them off their lands. They carried deadly diseases that spread to the native population. Approximately 300,000 Native Americans had lived in California before European settlers arrived.

Thousands of people worked in mines during the California Gold Rush.

By 1870, their population had been reduced to approximately 30,000 people.

Gold mining did not prove to be very prosperous. Only a few miners became wealthy. Later, the development of new industries would bring more wealth to the region.

NEW INDUSTRIES

In 1862, Congress passed the Pacific Railway Act. By 1869, a railroad connected the West and East Coasts.

MORMON SETTLEMENT IN UTAH

Mormonism is a religious belief. Joseph Smith founded Mormonism in the 1830s. Mormon communities grew in Ohio and Missouri. But many non-Mormons disliked the religion. They fought against Mormons and burned Mormon properties. Many Mormons moved from Missouri to Illinois in 1839. But they still could not find acceptance. Thousands of Mormons left the area in 1846. They settled in Utah's Great Salt Lake valley. Today, more than 2 million Mormons live in Utah. Their faith is a central part of their identities.

The railway line allowed the country to grow.

Jobs in logging camps and sawmills led people to the states of Washington, Oregon, and Idaho in the early 1900s. During World War II, the US government built manufacturing plants and bases in the West. Approximately half a million people came to Los Angeles to build ships for the military. By the 1960s, there were more people in California than in any other state.

Today, there are many different industries in the West. Cities such as Seattle, Washington; San Jose, California; and Denver, Colorado, are centers of US technology. Aerospace helps the economy of Colorado. More than 400 aerospace companies operate in the state. Many people move to Colorado to work in science and space research.

EXPLORE ONLINE

Chapter Two focuses on how the western region of the United States developed. The website below looks at how settlement and the railroad affected Native American tribes. Find a sentence or two from this website that relates to the information in the chapter. Does it support the information in Chapter Two? Or does it add a new piece of evidence? What can you learn from this website?

NATIVE AMERICANS AND THE TRANSCONTINENTAL RAILROAD
abdocorelibrary.com/exploring-west

CHAPTER
THREE

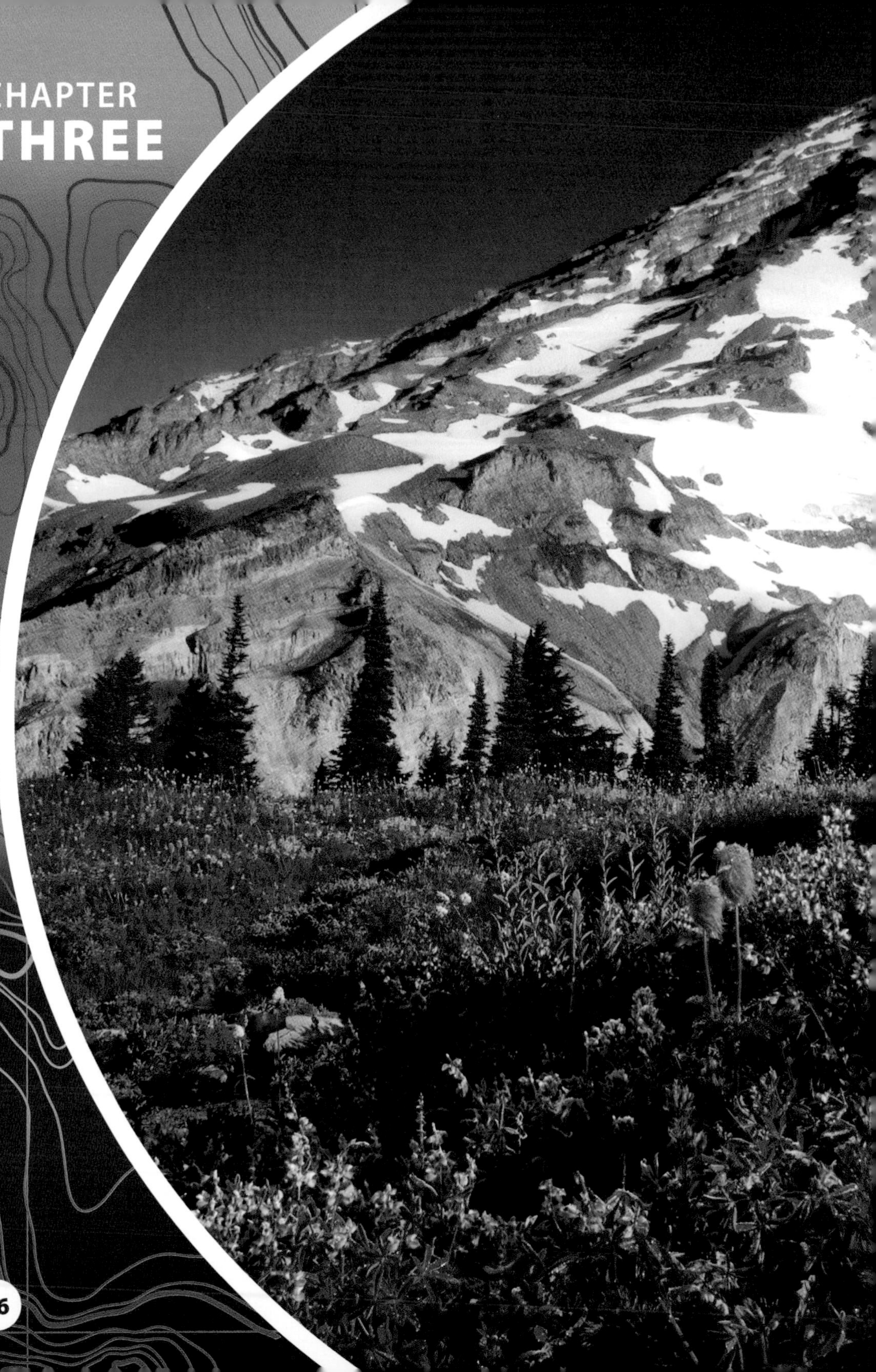

FAMOUS LANDMARKS

The West encompasses varied landscapes along with many natural and man-made features. Large mountain ranges cover this region. The Rocky Mountains are the longest mountain chain in North America. The range begins in Alaska. It crosses through western Canada and stretches south to New Mexico. Mount Elbert in Colorado is the highest peak in the chain. It is 14,433 feet (4,399 m) tall.

The Cascade Mountains run north to south from British Columbia in Canada to California. Mount Rainier in Washington is the tallest peak

Mount Rainier in Washington is part of the Cascade Mountain Range.

in this range. It is also the tallest volcano in the lower 48 states. The Puyallup Tribe in Washington State tells a story about the volcano. In the story, the volcano speaks to a man. It says that its water will flow when he dies.

THE GREAT ONE

Alaska is home to the tallest mountain in North America. It is called Denali. The word comes from a Native American language called Athabaskan. It means "the high one" or "the great one." The peak is 20,310 feet (6,190 m) tall. The mountain is in Denali National Park. Denali has an important role in the creation story of the Koyukon Athabascan people. They tell that the mountaintop was once the crest of a wave that formed during a great flood.

NATURAL MONUMENTS

Devils Tower is a famous landmark in Wyoming. It is a butte, or a hill with a flat top. Devils Tower and the land around it are sacred to tribes such as the Lakota.

Red stone bridges and arches in Utah are part of Arches National Park. There are more than 2,000 stone arches in the park. The Landscape Arch is the longest natural arch in the world.

Approximately 10,000 years ago, ancestors of Native Americans lived in this area. The Ute people came into this area in approximately 1300 CE. The word *Utah* is from the Ute language. It means "people of the mountain."

PERSPECTIVES

MAUNA KEA

Mauna Kea is an inactive volcano in Hawaii. It rises approximately 13,800 feet (4,206 m) above sea level. The night skies are usually cloud free because of the dry climate. This has attracted astronomers. There are more telescopes on Mauna Kea than on any other mountain in the world. There are plans to build one of the world's largest telescopes on Mauna Kea. But not everyone is pleased by this idea. Some native Hawaiians are concerned about the observatories. For them, the mountain is a sacred site. They believe that it is the home of Poliahu. She is the goddess of snow. If development continues, they worry that their cultural resources will be lost forever.

The Golden Gate Bridge in San Francisco, California, is an iconic landmark.

MAN-MADE LANDMARKS

The West contains some of the best-known man-made

landmarks in the United States. The Golden Gate Bridge

is a famous suspension bridge in California. It crosses the channel between San Francisco Bay and the Pacific Ocean. The Hoover Dam is also a great engineering landmark. It is on the state borders of Nevada and Arizona. The dam controls flood water from the Colorado River. It provides water to millions of acres of farmland in Nevada, Arizona, and California.

FURTHER EVIDENCE

Chapter Three looks at a few famous landmarks in the West. It describes the importance of some of these landmarks to native peoples. What was one of the chapter's main points? What evidence supports this point? The article at the website below discusses Athabascan culture on lands that are now part of Denali National Park. Does the article support Chapter Three's main point? Or does it add a new piece of evidence?

DENALI NATIONAL PARK AND PRESERVE

abdocorelibrary.com/exploring-west

CHAPTER FOUR

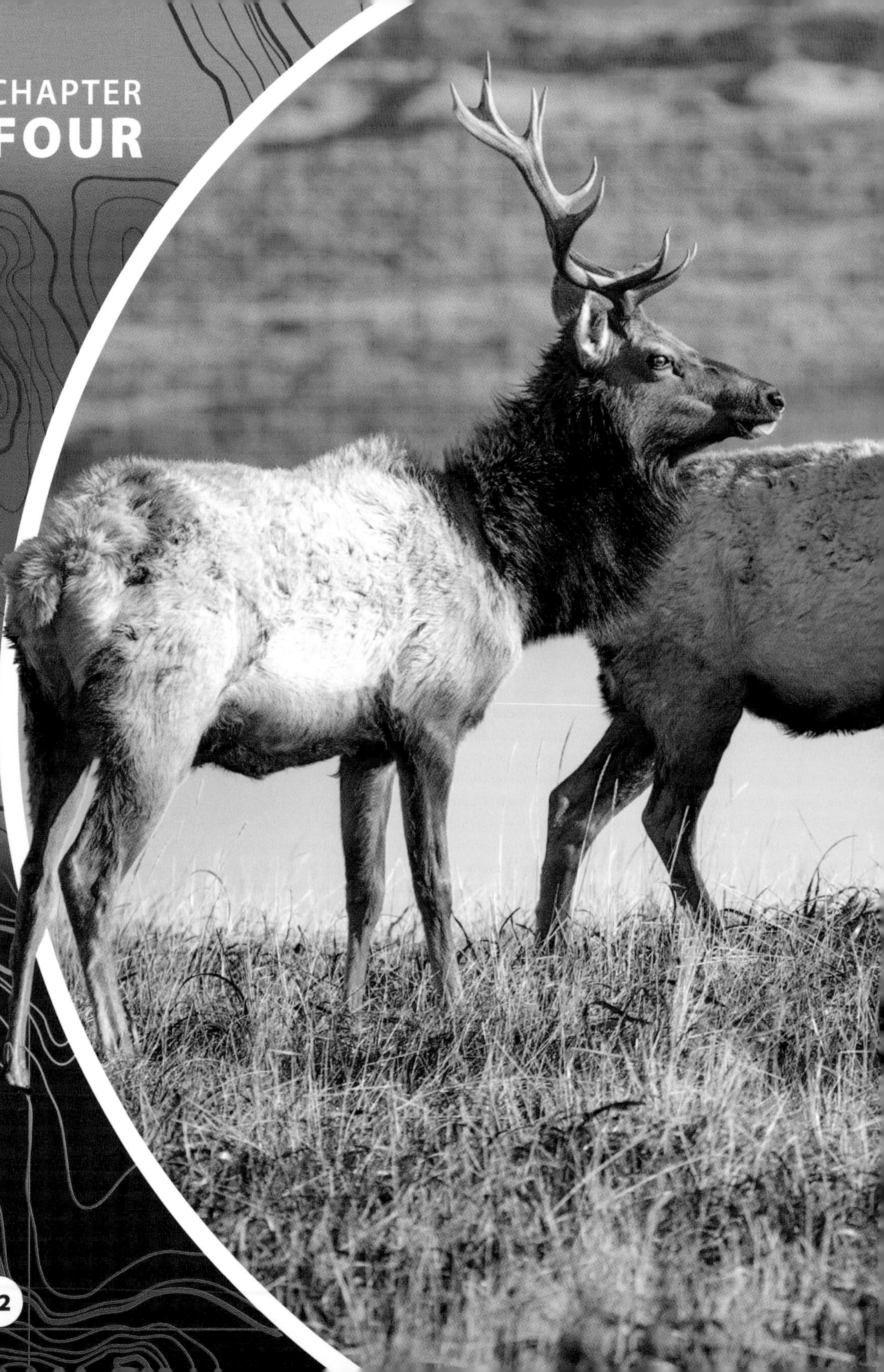

PLANTS AND ANIMALS

Many species of plants and animals have adapted to life in the West. Alaska is home to the largest population of bald eagles in the United States. Biologists believe there are approximately 30,000 bald eagles in the state. Many of these eagles flock to the Chilkat River. They feed on salmon that migrate to the river to lay eggs.

Large mammals including antelopes, elk, and bears are also found in the West. Some of these animals, such as the tule elk, live only in this region. Sea lions, seals, otters, and porpoises live near the coastline. Each winter,

Tule elk live on grasslands in California.

BIGHORN SHEEP

Bighorn sheep live in the western United States and in Canada. They are the state animal of Colorado. These sheep have huge, curled horns. Their horns can weigh as much as 30 pounds (14 kg). Bighorns live in large herds. Rocky Mountain bighorns are good at climbing. They use the cliffs to escape from predators. They are prey for animals such as cougars, wolves, and coyotes.

orca whales swim south along the coast of Alaska to warmer waters off the coast of Mexico.

THE GREAT PLAINS

The Great Plains are flat, grassy lands. They cover a large part of the central United States and Canada.

Lizards and small animals such as prairie dogs live on the plains. Prairie dogs live in large groups, or towns. Their excellent hearing helps them to avoid being caught by hawks and golden eagles.

Pronghorn antelope and bison also live on the plains. They graze on the short grass. Large herds of bison once roamed on the plains. But they gradually

Prairie dogs live throughout the Great Plains.

disappeared when pioneers overhunted them for sport. Today, Yellowstone National Park in Wyoming has the largest wild herd of bison in the United States. More than 5,500 bison are in this herd.

PLANTS OF THE WEST

Trees as tall as skyscrapers grow in the West. The redwood and giant sequoia trees of northern California are the tallest and largest trees in the world. The Hyperion redwood holds the record for the tallest tree. It is 379 feet (115 m) tall. Farther south, the spiky Joshua Tree grows in the Mojave Desert. This desert is in southern California and parts of Nevada. The Joshua Tree can live more than 150 years.

More than 2,500 species of plants are native to Hawaii. The ohai is a red or yellow flowering plant. Hawaiians string the ohai into necklaces called leis. Some Hawaiian plants were brought to the islands by Polynesians starting in 400 CE. These plants included taro, coconut, sugarcane, and banana. The state tree of Hawaii is the candlenut tree, or kukui. It was also brought to Hawaii by these settlers.

STRAIGHT TO THE
SOURCE

In 1871, a writer for *Scribner's Monthly* visited Yosemite National Park in California. In "A Visit to the Great Yo-Semite," the author wrote about seeing the Mariposa Grove of giant sequoia trees for the first time:

> *We are soon in the Mariposa grove. Who can picture, in language or on canvas, the thrilling and intense surprise when the eye first looks upon this marvelous scene! Long vistas of forest shades, formed by immense trunks of trees, stretch far away . . . while one hears ever the mysterious moaning and whispering of the great pines and firs. . . . One mighty tree that had fallen by fire and been burned out, into which we walked for a long distance, we found to be inhabited; a grizzly had made his nest there.*

> Source: J. S. "A Visit to the Great Yo-Semite." *Cornell University Library, Making of America Digital Collection*. Scribner's Monthly, August 1871. Web. Accessed April 18, 2017.

Consider Your Audience

Take a close look at this passage. Think about how you could share this information with another audience, such as your friends. Try writing a blog post that shares this information. How is your approach different from the original text, and why?

CHAPTER FIVE

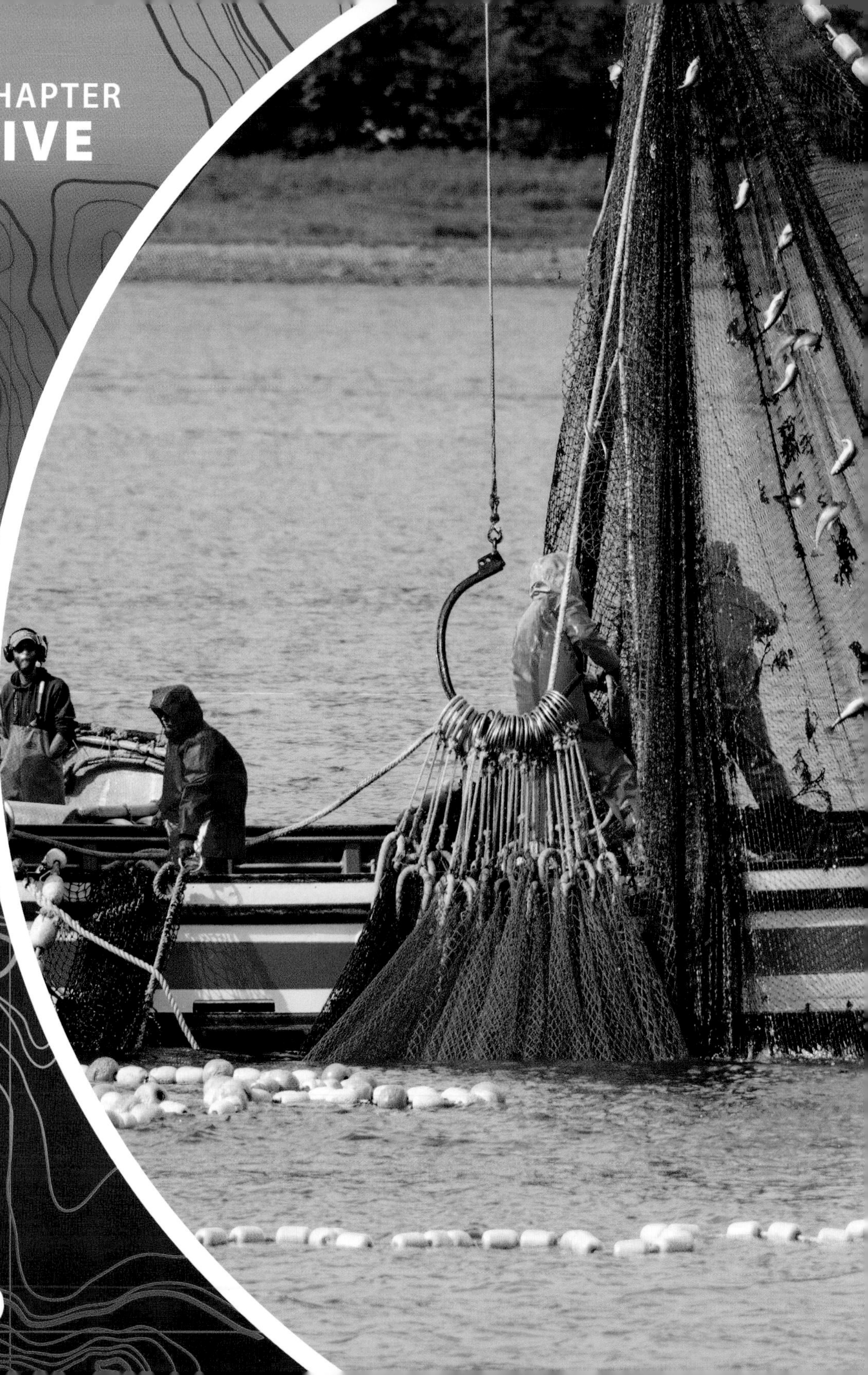

WORK IN THE WEST

People in the West work in a variety of industries. Many have jobs in agriculture. There are approximately 800,000 farmworkers in California. Farming is a major industry there. It brings in approximately $50 billion to the state each year. California grows more than half of all the fruits, vegetables, and nuts in the United States. There are many farms in California's Central Valley. Almonds, walnuts, rice, and tomatoes are its main crops.

Commercial fishing is also important along the coast. Fishers in Oregon catch crab, shrimp, tuna, and salmon. Fishing brings in

Fishers catch salmon off the coast of Alaska.

OREGON AGRICULTURE

There are more than 34,000 farms and ranches in Oregon. The Willamette Valley has some of the best soil in Oregon. Farmers harvest more than 170 different crops in the valley. They grow raspberries, blueberries, and wine grapes. Christmas tree farming is also important. Oregon produces the most Christmas trees in the United States. More than half of the trees it grows are sold in California.

more than $136 million each year to Oregon alone. Fishing is also a top industry in Alaska. Fishers in Alaska catch 40 percent of the world's salmon harvest. In Hawaii, fishers catch many types of shellfish, such as lobsters.

TOURISM

The West attracts tourists from around the world. There are plenty of beaches, national parks, and famous attractions to enjoy. More than 70 million visitors come to Colorado each year. Hikers and rafters can explore trails and rivers. Some visitors enjoy the state's ski resorts.

AGRICULTURE IN
CALIFORNIA

This graph shows the top agricultural products in California in 2015. Which crops bring in the most money for the state? What does the information tell you about agriculture in the state?

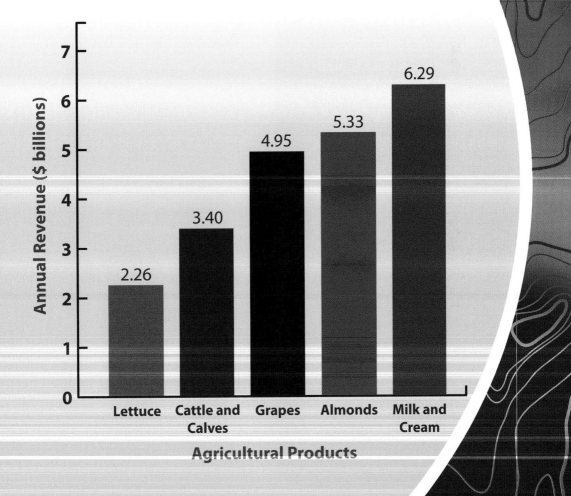

ENTERTAINMENT JOBS

Hollywood, California, has been the center of the entertainment industry since the early 1900s. The industry brings in $47 billion for the state's economy each year. Web-based television production is one of the fastest-growing entertainment sectors in Los Angeles. Kevin Klowden is an economist in California. In 2015, he explained why web-based television production does well in Los Angeles: "People are basing their operations here because this [is] where the talent is—the writers, actors and directors. It's really helping to reinforce the role of L.A. as the content center."

Tourism is important to California's economy. More than 250 million people visit the state each year. Los Angeles has lively neighborhoods and tours of movie studios. Disneyland California is one of the best-known attractions. There are large parades, fireworks, and rides. Tourism also draws people to Hawaii. It is the largest creator of jobs on the island. Visitors can go to one of the island's national

Keystone Resort is one of the most popular skiing destinations in Colorado.

parks. Hawaii Volcanoes National Park has 150 miles (241 km) of trails. There are volcanic craters, deserts, and rain forests to see.

TECHNOLOGY

Technology is another major industry in the West. In 2016, Utah added more tech jobs than anywhere else in the United States. In Washington, technology also helps the economy. It brings in more than $600 billion for the state each year. Companies such as Amazon and Microsoft have offices there. Microsoft creates software for computers. More than 40,000 people work for Microsoft in Washington.

California's computer industry is based in the San Francisco Bay area. This part of the state is known as Silicon Valley. Thousands of technology companies have their headquarters in the area. Twitter, Netflix, Facebook, and Google have offices there. Apple and Google are the largest employers. Computer engineers from all over the United States come to work for these tech companies.

Google's headquarters are in Mountain View, California.

CHAPTER
SIX

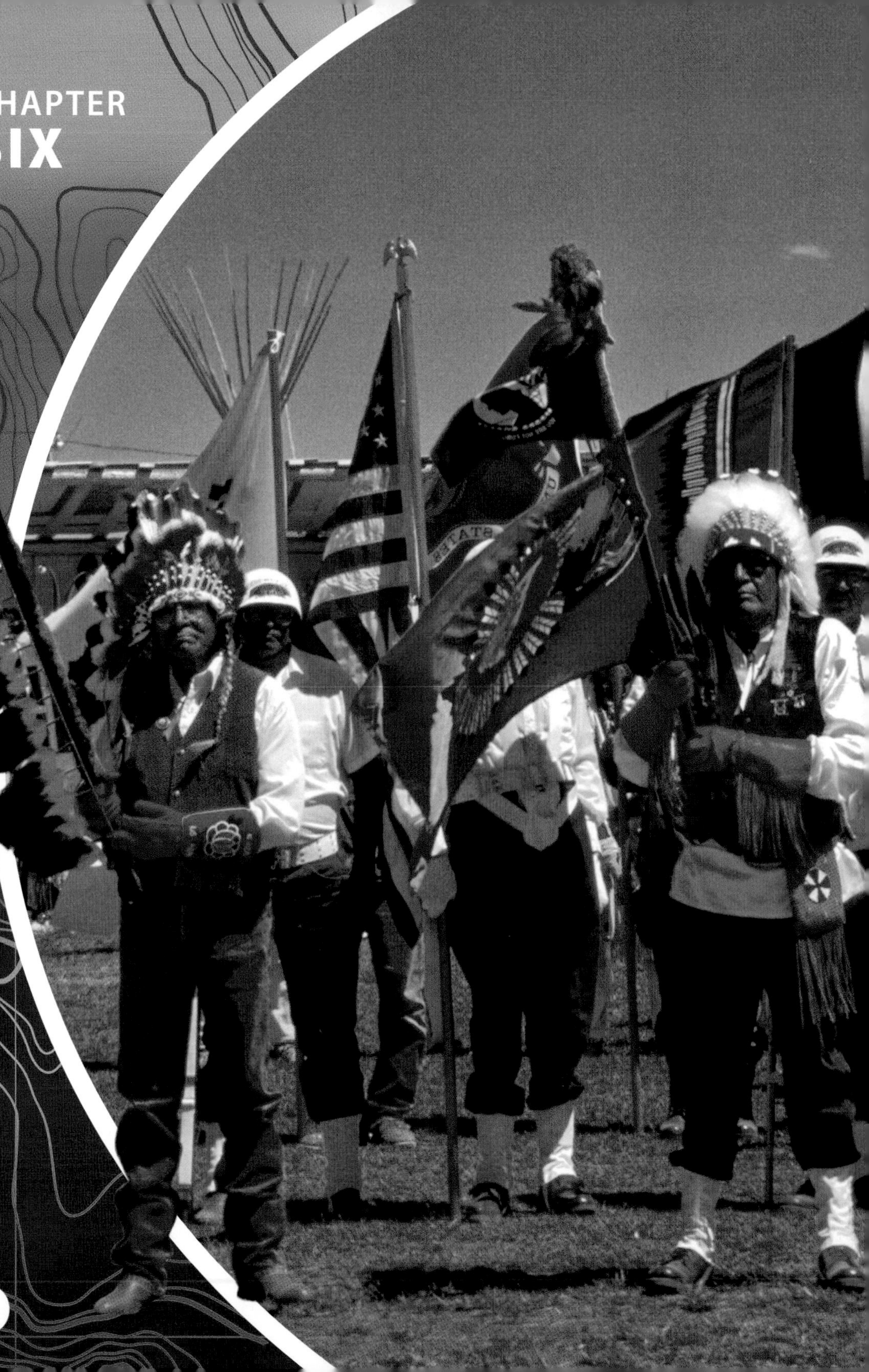

PEOPLES AND CULTURES

People from many different backgrounds have settled in the West. Both native and immigrant communities influence the cultures of the West.

More than half of all Native American nations are in the West. There are 12 Native American tribes in the state of Montana. The Blackfeet Nation in Montana includes more than 15,000 members. It is the largest Native American nation in the West.

Blackfeet war veterans march at a powwow in Browning, Montana.

SPANISH SPEAKERS

Many residents of the West can trace their roots to Mexico. Many also have their roots in South America. Nearly 15 million Spanish-speaking people live in California. The city of Los Angeles is home to the largest Mexican population in the West. One of the largest events held there is Dia de los Muertos, or Day of the Dead. On this day, people celebrate their ancestors with music and prayers.

ASIAN COMMUNITIES

Asians and Asian Americans are also a large demographic in the West. In the 1970s, many people from Southeast Asia came to settle in California. The largest group of immigrants was from Vietnam. The Vietnam War (1954–1975) had just ended. Communist North Vietnam had taken over South Vietnam. Many Vietnamese people feared communism. They journeyed across the Pacific Ocean to the United States on boats.

A DANISH VILLAGE

In 1911, three Danish settlers founded a town in California. They called it Solvang. The town's name means "sunny field" in Danish. The men placed ads in papers to attract more Danish people to the area. Solvang's Danish history is still a part of the town. Tourists come to see the Danish-style homes and windmills. Each September, the town hosts a festival called Danish Days. It includes folk dancers, Danish music, and parades.

Today, approximately 189,000 Vietnamese Americans live in Orange County. The county has the largest group of Vietnamese people outside of Vietnam. The city of Garden Grove is nicknamed Little Saigon. The name comes from the largest city in Vietnam, which was once called Saigon. The close-knit city is home to more than 4,000 Vietnamese-American stores, restaurants, and other businesses.

Since the early 1900s, people from the Philippines have also settled in the West. They are the largest Asian group in Alaska, California, Hawaii, Idaho, Montana, Nevada, Washington, and Wyoming. In the city of San Diego, California, Filipinos are the third-largest ethnic group.

Today, people continue to move to the western United States. They come looking for jobs, challenges, and opportunity. Many are attracted by the West's natural spaces. They want to be able to hike, bike, ski, or swim all year long.

STRAIGHT TO THE
SOURCE

Jim Hinch was a journalist for the *Orange County Register*. In 2012, he wrote about the history of Orange County's Little Saigon:

> *Approximately 3 million people who identify themselves as Vietnamese now live outside Vietnam. For older members of that diaspora, Orange County's Little Saigon is a powerful symbol of Vietnamese resilience and success. Just the name "Saigon" is a reminder of a pre-Communist era, a demonstration that exiled Vietnamese can start over and thrive, no matter where they end up. For younger Vietnamese and Vietnamese Americans, Little Saigon is something more straightforward—a place to eat, to hear the latest pop sensation or to start a business that might go international. . . . Orange County's Little Saigon is home to . . . more than 10 percent of all Vietnamese in America.*

> Source: Jim Hinch. "O.C.'s Saigon? Nothing Little About It." *Orange County Register*. Orange County Register, November 5, 2012. Web. Accessed April 18, 2017.

What's the Big Idea?
Read the text carefully. What is the author's main point? What evidence does the author give to back up this view? Write down two or three pieces of evidence given in the article.

FAST FACTS

- Total Area: 1.2 million square miles (3.1 million sq km)

- Population: Approximately 67 million people

- Largest City: Los Angeles, California

- Largest State by Population: California

- Smallest State by Population: Wyoming

- Largest State by Land Size: Alaska

- Smallest State by Land Size: Washington

- Highest Point: Mount Whitney in California, 14,494 feet (4,418 m) above sea level

- Lowest Point: Badwater Basin in California, 282 feet (86 m) below sea level

- Nickname: Utah is nicknamed the beehive state because it reminds people that the early pioneers had to work hard to survive.

- Landmark: At 11,333 feet (3,454 m) tall, Colorado's Grand Mesa is one of the largest mountains with a flat top in the world.

- Water: There are more than 3 million lakes and approximately 100,000 glaciers in the state of Alaska.

STOP AND
THINK

You Are There

This book covers the history, landmarks, and culture of the West. Imagine that you are planning a trip to the West. Write a journal entry about your trip. Which places would you most like to visit? What additional information would you like to learn about those areas?

Say What?

Studying the western region of the United States can mean learning new vocabulary. Find five words in this book you had never heard before. Use the glossary or a dictionary to find out what they mean. Then write the meanings in your own words. Use each word in a new sentence.

Dig Deeper

After reading this book, what questions do you still have about the western region of the United States? With an adult's help, find a few reliable sources that can help you answer your questions. Write a paragraph about what you learned.

Another View

This book explores the effects of westward expansion on Native American tribes. As you know, every source is different. Ask an adult to help you find other sources on this period. Compare the new source to this book. What is the point of view of each author? How are they similar and why? How are they different and why?

GLOSSARY

aerospace
a technology industry that is involved in flight and space research

communism
a system in which people produce goods that are meant to be owned and shared equally

culture
the customs, beliefs, and traditions held by a group of people

diaspora
a group of people who live far from their homeland or their ancestors' homeland

nation
a group of people who share a language, culture, and ancestry

Polynesian
a person from one of more than 1,000 islands in the Pacific Ocean

reservation
an area of land set aside by the federal government for use by a Native American tribe

suspension bridge
a bridge in which the weight of a roadway is supported by two or more cables that pass over towers and are anchored to the ground

territory
an area of land that belongs to or is controlled by a country

ONLINE
RESOURCES

To learn more about the western region of the United States, visit our free resource websites below.

Visit **abdocorelibrary.com** for free Common Core resources for teachers and students, including vetted activities, multimedia, and booklinks, for deeper subject comprehension.

Visit **abdobooklinks.com** for free additional online weblinks for further learning. These links are routinely monitored and updated to provide the most current information available.

LEARN
MORE

Bell, Samantha S. *Traditional Stories of the California Nations.* Minneapolis, MN: Abdo, 2017.

Byers, Ann. *Life as a Homesteader in the American West.* New York, NY: Cavendish Square, 2017.

INDEX

About the Author

Anita Yasuda is the author of many books for children. She enjoys writing biographies, books about science and social studies, and chapter books. Anita lives with her family in Huntington Beach, California, where you can find her on most days walking her dog along the shore.